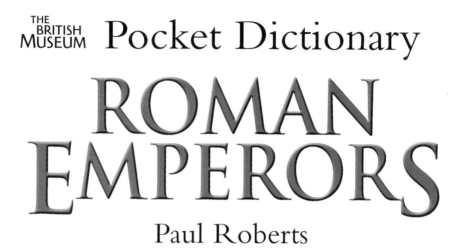

THE BRITISH MUSEUM **Pocket Dictionary**

ROMAN EMPERORS

Paul Roberts

THE BRITISH MUSEUM PRESS

Published in 2006 by British Museum Press
A division of the British Museum Company Ltd
38 Russell Square, London WC1B 3QQ

ISBN-10: 0-7141-3116-4
ISBN-13: 978-0-7141-3116-0

Paul Roberts has asserted the right to be
identified as the author of this work.

A catalogue record for this title is available from
the British Library.

Designed and typeset by Proof Books.
Printed in Singapore.

CONTENTS

A–Z list of Emperors

Introduction

The emperors of Rome are very familiar to us today from books, television and cinema. But who were the real emperors?

Rome did not always have emperors. Legend said that Rome was founded in 753 BC by Romulus, who became Rome's first king. Rome was ruled by kings until 509 BC, when the last king was expelled and Rome became a Republic. The Republic lasted for five hundred years but Rome's conquests stretched the Republic too far and it collapsed in civil war. Out of the ruins came Octavian, who became Augustus, the first emperor, in 27 BC.

The emperors had absolute control over the empire and its citizens, and their personal power was immense. An emperor was head of state, head of the state religion and commander of the armed forces (the title 'emperor' comes from the Latin word *imperator*, meaning 'commander').

In the five centuries between Augustus and the last emperor Romulus 'Augustulus', the throne was occupied by about sixty 'legal' emperors and more than twenty-five other pretenders and usurpers. The emperors ranged from great statesmen and generals to philosophers, murderers and madmen. This book looks at twenty-seven of these extraordinary people.

Augustus (Emperor 27 BC – AD 14)

Many think that Julius Caesar was the first emperor, but he was really a *dictator*. He stopped Rome's civil wars but was assassinated on the Ides (15th) of March 44 BC. Octavian, his great-nephew and adopted son, avenged him and defeated Mark Antony and Cleopatra at the battle of Actium in 31 BC. Octavian became the undisputed master of Rome and was named Augustus.

Augustus was the first and one of the greatest of Rome's emperors. He gave the Roman world a much-needed period of unity, peace and stability. He was ambitious and at times ruthless, but also very intelligent, and he created a new Rome. He completely re-organised the government of Rome and the empire and to emphasise his imperial authority he put his image everywhere, on coins, metal and

A bronze head of Augustus, the first emperor of Rome.

6

stone sculptures, even jewellery. He strengthened the empire's frontiers and added new areas, including Egypt, Austria and parts of Germany and Spain. The empire prospered, the cities grew and the economy boomed. Augustus rebuilt or renovated all Rome's major buildings including the Senate House, the Temple of Julius Caesar and the Forum of Augustus. As Augustus said, 'I found Rome a city of brick and left it a city of marble ...' All over the empire the same transformation occurred. The arts flourished and artists created beautiful mosaics and wall paintings, jewellery, sculptures, and fine tableware of gold, silver, pottery and glass for the bustling markets.

The Portland Vase. This beautiful cameo glass vase shows the skill of craftsmen in Augustan Rome.

Augustus indeed changed the world, and poets such as Vergil and Horace praised him, but who could succeed him? His chosen successors, such as Agrippa his son-in-law and deputy, and his grandsons Gaius and Lucius, all died before him. He finally adopted Tiberius, the son of his second wife Livia. When Augustus died in AD 14, he was buried in Rome in a round mausoleum. Outside were inscribed his *Res Gestae* – a huge list of his many achievements.

The Pont du Gard aqueduct in France. Bridges, roads and aqueducts criss-crossed Augustus' empire.

Tiberius (Emperor AD 14 – 37)

Augustus adopted Tiberius as his successor in AD 4, partly through the influence and intrigues of Tiberius' mother Livia (Augustus' second wife), and partly because of the early deaths of all the other potential successors.

After Augustus' death no one knew how power could be transferred, but eventually the Senate and the army persuaded Tiberius to take the throne. Although Tiberius was a successful general and had fought across the empire from Armenia to Spain, he never had the good relationship with the Senate and the people that Augustus had enjoyed. He did not trust the Senate, allowing it very little involvement in affairs of state. Tiberius did not create beautiful buildings for the people, or give them the games and festivals they had come to expect. This gave him a (well-earned) reputation for meanness.

Tiberius also liked to hide himself away. During the reign of Augustus he spent several years on the Greek island of Rhodes, and he spent the last years of his reign on the Italian island of Capri. His extravagance and private excesses in the Villa Iovis (Jupiter's Villa) became infamous. He often played host to the young Gaius (Caligula) and much of Gaius' outrageous behaviour was probably learnt during these visits.

Golden decorative plaque from a sword.
It shows Tiberius offering the glory of his
victories to his step-father Augustus.

8

With Tiberius away from Rome, power passed into the hands of Sejanus, the ambitious and brutal head of the emperor's bodyguard, the Praetorian Guard, set up by Augustus. He wielded this power mercilessly and killed hundreds of people on false charges of treason, including members of the imperial family. Sejanus was finally executed, and was replaced by another powerful Praetorian, Macro.

Like Augustus, Tiberius saw his planned successors die before their time. The deaths of his son Drusus and nephew Germanicus left him with little option but to adopt Caligula. Rumours said that Caligula himself hastened the old man's death at the Villa Iovis in AD 37, holding a pillow over Tiberius' face.

Marble bust of Tiberius as a young man, before his later unpopularity and self-imposed exile on Capri.

Caligula (Gaius) (Emperor AD 37 – 41)

Gaius, the great-grandson of Augustus, was the son of the immensely popular prince Germanicus, and spent much of his childhood on campaign with the army. The soldiers nicknamed him *Caligula* ('Little boots') on account of his miniature military boots and, to his annoyance, the nickname stuck.

Caligula's mother and brothers were executed for plotting against Tiberius, but Caligula became the emperor's favourite. He had a cruel streak and was an avid fan of public executions and gladiatorial fights. Tiberius recognised Caligula's dark side, remarking 'I've raised a viper at Rome's bosom'.

After Tiberius' death, Caligula was enormously popular at first among the Senators and the people. He held lavish games, spectacularly illuminated the

Coin of Caligula as Zeus. The Romans adopted the custom of treating the emperor as a living god from the Greeks.

centre of Rome and even threw a bridge of boats across part of the Bay of Naples. But his popularity decreased as his personal behaviour became more and more bizarre. He scandalised Rome with a string of affairs with women and men, and was far too fond of his own sister Drusilla. He declared himself a god, and had heated conversations with Capitoline Jupiter, the supreme deity of Rome. He spent a fortune on luxuries, including banquets, enormous pleasure barges and even a marble stable and gold food for his favourite horse. His extravagance emptied the treasury, so he raised money through higher taxes and extortion. He became increasingly isolated and saw plots and treason everywhere, particularly in the Senate. He executed suspects and took their fortunes.

He treated the ordinary people no better. On one occasion he removed the *velarium* (sun-shade) from the gladiatorial arena, so that the people baked in the hot sun. Once he muttered that he wished all Romans had only one neck (all the easier to cut). Eventually he went too far and was assassinated by his own guards during an interval at the games, passing into history as one of the cruellest, most dangerous emperors.

Bronze statuette of Jupiter, king of the Roman gods. Caligula used to argue with him in his temple on the Capitoline hill in Rome.

Claudius (Emperor AD 41 – 54)

Claudius was the son of Drusus (Tiberius' brother) and Antonia, the daughter of Mark Antony. Although tall, handsome and well built, Claudius had disabilities, including a stammer, a facial tic and a tendency to stumble. Augustus and Livia kept him out of the public gaze by denying him public office and restricting his appearances at games and festivals. So he spent his time in bars and gambling dens, though in quieter moments he liked to write books on history and linguistics.

After the assassination of Caligula, Claudius became emperor, almost by chance, after a soldier discovered him hiding behind a curtain in the imperial palace. While the Senate dithered over how to restore the Republic, the Praetorian Guard, the emperor's bodyguards, proclaimed him emperor.

Cameo of Claudius in military uniform. Claudius conquered Britain and brought it into the Roman empire.

Claudius immediately embarked on major public works. Two new aqueducts brought water to the city and a new deep-water harbour was created at Ostia, the port of Rome, to accommodate the huge wheat barges from Egypt and North Africa. Claudius knew the importance to the poor of 'bread and circuses', because he was once jostled by a hungry mob in the Forum. As for circuses, he loved a spectacle. Before a mock sea battle, men shouted the famous words 'Hail Caesar! We who are about to die salute you!', but Claudius' reply 'Or not, as the case may be!' resulted in a near-mutiny. A more successful military achievement came with the conquest of Britain in AD 43, in which the future emperor Vespasian campaigned.

Claudius was unlucky in love and had several wives including the treacherous Messalina and finally his own niece Agrippina. He adopted one of her children, Nero, and the empire passed to Nero when Claudius was murdered in AD 54. It seems likely that Agrippina herself was involved in the murder, putting poison in a dish of mushrooms – one of Claudius' favourite dishes.

The Porta Maggiore in Rome. It still carries part of an aqueduct built by Claudius.

Nero (Emperor AD 54 – 68)

When the teenage Nero became emperor, the public adored this stylish playboy prince, with his lavish banquets and his passion for chariot-racing. The Senate liked his promise of government by consent. The army welcomed the extra money he gave them, and in return delivered military successes, such as the defeat of Boudicca in Britain in AD 61.

Nero always preferred the arts to ruling the empire. He played instruments and composed and recited poetry in Greek and Latin, always at great length. Doors were barred to stop people leaving his concerts, and even an earthquake during his stage debut at Naples could not stop him. His private life, however, was far from amusing. He poisoned Britannicus, Claudius' son, then had his own mother, Agrippina,

Bronze statuette of Nero. In this pose he resembles his hero, the Macedonian commander Alexander the Great.

murdered. He exiled and then executed his first wife Octavia, and kicked his second wife Poppaea to death when she was pregnant.

In July AD 64 the great fire of Rome swept away much of the city. Nero was criticised for doing nothing to prevent it, so he blamed the Christians and executed them in various ways, even using them as human torches. He rebuilt some fire-ravaged areas, but used the rest to build the *Domus Aurea* (Golden House). This was his luxuriously decorated pleasure palace, set in hundreds of acres of parks and gardens, with a vast lake, where the Colosseum now stands. A colossal statue of the emperor, (after which the Colosseum was named), stood at the entrance of the palace. Later Nero embarked on a tour of Greece where he took part in games and festivals, and even drove a ten-horse chariot at Olympia. He returned to Rome with dozens of looted works of art to fill his new home.

Nero funded his expenditure through executions and extortion, and this led to conspiracies and ultimately a major rebellion led by Galba the governor of southern Spain. In summer AD 68 Nero fled Rome in disguise and finally committed suicide, crying 'What an artist dies in me'.

The theatre of Dionysus in Athens. Nero toured the sanctuaries, theatres and stadia of Greece, demanding prizes and stealing works of art.

Vespasian (Emperor AD 69 – 79)

Vespasian was born near Rieti in the Sabine Hills above Rome. His portraits show a square face and a heavy, lined brow. His dynasty was named after his family, the Flavians.

In the army he helped to conquer Britain and was then sent, together with his son Titus, to put down the Jewish revolt in Judaea. Vespasian lay low after the suicide of Nero in AD 68, while three rival emperors, Galba, Otho and Vitellius tore Rome and the empire apart. But Titus won over the eastern legions for his father, and Vespasian was proclaimed emperor when Vitellius was assassinated.

Vespasian first restored the rule of law and brought the Senate back to full numbers, even pardoning old enemies. Then he

Marble head of Vespasian, showing him with his characteristic frown.

rebuilt many of Rome's damaged buildings, including the Temple of Jupiter Optimus Maximus on the Capitol. This was expensive, but in AD 70 Titus took Jerusalem and brought back huge quantities of gold. This was displayed in a mighty triumphal procession, parts of which are shown on the Arch of Titus in the Forum. The booty funded two major new projects. First was an immense forum and 'Temple of Peace', filled with sculptures from Nero's palace, as well as relics from Jerusalem, such as the *menorah* or great seven-branched candlestick. Second was the construction of the immense *Amphitheatrum Flavium* or Colosseum, the amphitheatre that has come to symbolise Rome.

All of this was expensive, even with Judaea's gold, so Vespasian had to raise taxes. Even public urinals were taxed. When Titus was critical,

The *Amphitheatrum Flavium*, or Colosseum, built by Vespasian with the gold from Jerusalem.

Vespasian held some of the coins under Titus' nose and said 'do they smell any different?'. Vespasian was humorous even in dying, and referring to the trend of deifying deceased emperors, declared 'Heavens, I think I'm becoming a god!' Significantly there was no dispute over Vespasian's successor, since without consulting the Senate he had already chosen his son Titus.

Titus (Emperor AD 79 – 81)

Titus was born in Rome, in a poor tenement block that later became a tourist attraction. He was well-built and muscular and portraits show a very strong likeness to his father, Vespasian. They fought together to suppress the Jewish revolt in Judaea and in the chaos of AD 68-9 Titus held the eastern empire for his father. In AD 70, with Vespasian now emperor, Titus captured Jerusalem and returned to Rome in triumph.

Titus became his father's deputy and head of the Praetorian Guard. He had enormous power (and lots of enemies) because he dealt with banishments, accusations of treason and death warrants. He was married, but he had a very public affair with Queen Berenice of Judaea. All this made him very unpopular with many parts of Roman society.

Marble head of Titus, the loyal son and colleague of Vespasian.

Titus became emperor when Vespasian died in AD 79. He suddenly became very lenient, collaborated with the Senate, changed his luxurious lifestyle and cut all communication with Berenice. On 24 August AD 79 the volcano Mount Vesuvius erupted and destroyed the cities of Pompeii and Herculaneum. Titus poured his personal money into disaster relief, and when Rome was devastated by fire only weeks later Titus immediately set about rebuilding it. He was now seen as a generous, caring emperor, 'the love and delight of the whole human race' as the historian Suetonius says.

AD 80 saw the opening of the *Amphitheatrum Flavium* or Colosseum. This enormous arena, over 150 ft (48 m) high and

The Arch of Titus at the entrance to the Roman Forum. It commemorated Titus' triumph over Judaea.

600 ft (183 m) across, holding over 60,000 people, symbolised the power of Rome, the emperor and the Flavians. The opening games lasted for 100 days and thousands of gladiators and animals fought for the enjoyment of the crowd and the glory of the emperor. Nearby, over the deliberately-buried remains of the *Domus Aurea*, Titus built his huge public baths.

After only two years on the throne Titus suddenly died. He caught a fever on a journey to his country retreat in the Sabine hills and never recovered. His mysterious last words as he died were 'I have made only one mistake'.

Domitian (Emperor AD 81 – 96)

Domitian, Vespasian's younger son, was never part of the 'special relationship' between Vespasian and Titus, but was Titus' obvious successor. Domitian was acclaimed as emperor by the Praetorian Guard, and rewarded the army with a huge pay rise. He won important victories on the Rhine and Danube frontiers before turning to affairs in Rome. He set new high standards in the civil service and rigidly enforced high moral standards in public life. He executed four Vestal virgins (priestesses of Vesta) for breaking their vow of chastity. The senior Vestal was buried alive.

Domitian began major building programmes in Rome, creating or completing monuments, including a temple and an arch in the Forum to honour his father and brother, a stadium for Greek-style athletics (now the Piazza Navona), and a new Forum. This came to be known as the Forum of Nerva (Domitian's successor) after Domitian's death and disgrace. In the Forum Romanum Domitian erected a colossal mounted statue of himself, the largest statue in the Forum.

Bronze coin of Domitian from early in his reign.

The sunken 'Hippodrome' (in reality a colonnaded garden) of
Domitian's great palace on the Palatine Hill in Rome.

Early in his reign Domitian was popular, but after several rebellions and
assassination attempts he became increasingly intolerant and paranoid. He turned
away from the Senate and towards his own imperial court in his vast new palace
on the Palatine. It was divided into two main areas, the official *Domus Flavia* with
immense halls for banqueting and audiences, and the *Domus Augustana*, the
emperor's private residence, its corridors lined with reflective, assassin-proof
marble. Contemporary writers described the palace as unbelievably opulent.

Treason trials became commonplace and in AD 93 he unleashed a full-blown
reign of terror against his real and imagined enemies. Even the empress, Domitia,
feared for her life. Finally she joined a conspiracy to kill the emperor, and in
AD 96 he was assassinated by two of his trusted courtiers, one of whom had
hidden a knife in a false bandage wrapped round his arm.

Trajan (Emperor AD 98 – 117)

After the assassination of Domitian, the Senate selected Nerva, a respected military veteran, as emperor. He restored order and wisely adopted as his successor Trajan, a popular military commander.

Trajan was born near Seville in modern Spain and was the first emperor from a non-Italian family, underlining the increasing importance of the provinces. He and his wife Plotina lived a simple and harmonious life, though in private, like many emperors, he liked to drink and have boyfriends. In public he was devoted to improving the lives of his subjects. He increased the *alimenta* (free food for the

poor) and safeguarded the *annona* (the wheat supply from North Africa and Egypt), by building a great hexagonal deep-water harbour at Portus, an extension of the port of Claudius.

Although a strong ruler, Trajan was renowned for fairness and good government. This is seen in his correspondence with an imperial governor, the Younger Pliny, in which Trajan advocated a tolerant policy towards Christians. The Medieval writer Dante AlTumbleigheri thought he was the only pagan Roman emperor worthy of a place in his book *Paradiso*. Legends about his virtues were still told in the Middle Ages.

Bronze statuette of a Roman legionary soldier.
Under Trajan, the empire reached its greatest extent.

Trajan also extended the empire. He conquered Dacia (modern Romania) and defeated the powerful Persian empire in the east, occupying its homeland of Mesopotamia (modern Iraq). The booty from Dacia was used for a massive building project in Rome, the forum and markets of Trajan. This combined a vast piazza, a basilica, law courts, libraries, markets, offices and residential property in one huge complex in the very heart of Rome. The multi-storey covered arcade and Trajan's column, covered with carvings showing the Dacian wars, can still be seen.

While Trajan was campaigning in the east, the Jewish population in Cyrene (modern Libya) rebelled. He rushed back to deal with this very serious revolt, but died of a stroke. He was deified and his ashes were placed in the chamber at the base of Trajan's column.

Marble bust of Trajan, shown with a nude torso, in heroic Greek style.

Hadrian (Emperor AD 117 – 138)

Trajan chose Hadrian, one of his relatives and also of Spanish descent, to be his heir. Other emperors were content to stay in Rome when not at war, but Hadrian spent his reign travelling all over the empire.

He strengthened Rome's frontiers, by ordering work to start on Hadrian's Wall in Britain, for example, and he fixed the main boundaries of the empire at three great rivers, the Rhine in the west, the Danube in the centre and the Euphrates in the east.

When Hadrian wasn't travelling, he was building. In Rome he constructed the enormous Temple of Venus and Rome, his round

Bronze head of Hadrian, found in the River Thames in London.

Hadrian's Wall in the north of England, one of the many civil and military projects that Hadrian initiated throughout the empire.

mausoleum (now the Castel sant'Angelo) and the beautiful Pantheon with its domed roof. At Tivoli to the east of Rome, he built a vast villa, filled with works of art. He was very well-educated, and wrote poetry and an autobiography, though virtually nothing has survived. He was passionate about Greek culture and Greece, and built several beautiful buildings in Athens including Hadrian's Library and the Temple of Zeus. He even wore a Greek-style beard, and because of his love of Greece some Senators called him Graeculus (the little Greek). His passion, however, did not extend to his wife, Sabina, and he preferred his male lover, Antinous, deified by Hadrian after his mysterious death in the River Nile.

Hadrian also had a very dark side. At the beginning and end of his reign, there were numbers of unjustifiable executions, and he could also be obsessive. In his passion for architecture, he quarrelled so violently with the architect Apollodorus of Damascus, over plans for a new temple, that the architect was first banished and then murdered.

Hadrian adopted Aelius Caesar, who died, so he then adopted Antoninus Pius. Afterwards Hadrian fell seriously ill and retired to the seaside resort of Baiae on the Bay of Naples, where he died in AD 134.

Antoninus Pius

Antoninus was born near Rome into a wealthy aristocratic family, originally from southern France. Described as tall and handsome, with a warm, open character, he became a senior judge and was invited to be part of the imperial council. In AD 138 he was adopted by Hadrian, and when Hadrian died four months later, he became emperor.

At first he clashed with the Senate, which wouldn't deify Hadrian because it had disliked his autocratic style of government. But the Senate eventually gave in, after which relations between emperor and Senate blossomed. Antoninus was even awarded the title *Pius*, in recognition of his services to the state, its laws and religion.

His reign was relatively peaceful. There were some military operations, for example the suppression of a Jewish revolt in the Near East, but the most serious campaign took place in Britain. Here Antoninus put down a rebellion by the northern tribe, the Brigantes, and pushed Roman control beyond Hadrian's Wall, creating the 'Antonine Wall' in Scotland, between the rivers Forth and Clyde. When not on campaign, Antoninus (unlike Hadrian), preferred not to travel. Instead he spent his time in Rome or at his country villa at Lorium, nearby.

The empire reaped the benefits of peace. The cities and countryside prospered and the treasury overflowed with silver that was not being used to pay for costly wars. Antoninus personally used this time to ensure that the empire was governed firmly but fairly, by reforming the judiciary and the

civil service. In Rome he built a
temple to the deified Hadrian and
another in the Forum to his adored
wife Faustina, deified after her death in
AD 140. Antoninus was also deified after
he died peacefully at Lorium in AD 161,
at the ripe old age of 74.

Marble bust of Antoninus Pius.
Here he is wearing a military cloak,
but his reign was characterised by
peace and prosperity.

Marcus Aurelius (Emperor AD 161 – 180)

Born in his family's villa on the Caelian Hill in Rome, Marcus Aurelius was a thoughtful, sombre child. He was fascinated by philosophy and attended the lectures of the best philosophers in Rome.

He was taken into the imperial household by Hadrian, and was trained in sports and hunting, but always preferred philosophy. Eventually Marcus was adopted by Antoninus Pius, and married Antoninus' daughter Faustina the Younger. Together they had fourteen children.

When Antoninus died, Marcus made his cousin Lucius Verus joint emperor, and the two commanders made a powerful combination. In AD 165 they defeated the Persians, who had invaded Rome's ally, Armenia. They held a spectacular joint triumph at Rome, but celebrations were short-lived because plague, brought back by the army, tore through the city and then the empire, killing tens of thousands of people. The emperors were heading to confront barbarians who had burst into northern Italy when, in AD 169, Lucius died of a stroke. Marcus ruled alone, and campaigned from the Czech Republic to Hungary. Striking images from his wars are preserved on the 'Antonine' column in Rome.

Marcus made a clear division between military and civil power, and was measured and moderate in everything he did. He was also the author of a dozen volumes of *Meditations*, his thoughts on life. These earned him the title 'the philosopher emperor', and were popular well into the Middle Ages.

From AD 178 he campaigned on the Danube with his son Commodus, but fell ill and died in AD 180. He used his last words to encourage his courtiers to think of others, not of him.

Marble bust of Marcus Aurelius, the 'philosopher' emperor. He is shown as *Pontifex Maximus*, the high priest of the Roman state religion.

Commodus (Emperor AD 180 – 192)

Unlike most of the emperors of the second century, Commodus was not adopted, but was one of the (fourteen!) children of Marcus Aurelius and Faustina the Younger. He was famous for his good looks – and his golden blond hair.

He was also infamous for his cruelty. He started young, ordering a bath attendant to be thrown into the furnace because his bath was not hot enough. He was very fond of gladiatorial and animal sports, and rumours spread that his real father was a gladiator or that his mother had bathed in gladiator's blood before Commodus was conceived. He sometimes fought with men, but he also took on ferocious beasts, such as elephants or tigers. His favourite prey was the ostrich, and he liked to dress as Hercules, his

Marble bust of Commodus. Here he is impersonating the Greek hero Hercules, with club and lion skin.

patron deity, and slaughter dozens at a time. On one occasion in the arena he stood in front of the Senators' seats waggling the severed head of an ostrich in one hand and his bloody sword in the other. The message was clear: 'I can kill ostriches and I can kill you ...'

Commodus devoted himself to pleasures of all sorts in his villa on the Appian Way to the south of the city, and left affairs of state to trusted officials such as Perennis and Cleander. These became the most powerful people in the empire. Imperial offices and army commands were openly bought and sold and random executions were ordered. People became increasingly alarmed and began to plot against him. After one of these plots, Commodus' own sister Lucilla was executed. His excesses finally became too much. He was about to rename Rome 'Colonia Commodiana' after himself, and to lead the gladiators into the Colosseum dressed as a gladiator himself, when he was killed by one of his own entertainers, Narcissus. By command of the Senate he suffered *Damnatio Memoriae*: his statues were destroyed and his name was removed from official records and inscriptions.

Bronze gladiator's helmet. Commodus' appearances in the arena scandalised Rome.

Septimius Severus (Emperor AD 193 – 211)

Septimius was born in Leptis Magna in modern Libya, and was partly of native North African descent. It was said that he had quite dark skin and spoke Latin with a strong regional accent.

Septimius married a Syrian noblewoman, Julia Domna, and they had two children, Geta and the future emperor Caracalla. Septimius was governor of several provinces including Sicily, and then became commander of the Danube legions. When Commodus was murdered, Septimius' armies made him emperor at Carnuntum (near Vienna) and he marched on Rome. He dismissed the soldiers of the Praetorian Guard, who had already sold the empire twice, and replaced them with his own soldiers.

For three years he fought against usurpers from Britain to Turkey, and in AD 197 he finally re-united the empire. The following year he smashed the Persian empire, capturing the capital, Ctesiphon, and annexing the whole of Mesopotamia, just as Trajan had done a century earlier.

Marble statue of Septimius Severus in military uniform. This North African emperor spent much of his reign fighting.

The theatre of Leptis Magna, modern Libya. Septimius was born in Leptis, and when he became emperor he transformed it with fine buildings.

In Rome, Septimius was a very capable administrator and judge. Even so, he was first and foremost the army's man. He increased the number of legions to thirty-five, their greatest number ever, and he awarded the army large pay increases. Military service, not noble birth, was now the key to a wide range of senior civil positions, and this set the tone for the future.

He was one of the last of the great imperial builders. In Rome he rebuilt the fire-damaged Pantheon and the Portico of Octavia, and constructed the arch of Severus. In North Africa he transformed his home town of Leptis Magna into an imperial city with massive buildings including a forum and a basilica.

In AD 211 he was in Britain campaigning against the tribes in Scotland when he fell ill and died, with his family around him, at York.

Caracalla (Emperor AD 211 – 217)

On his death-bed Septimius told Caracalla and Geta to 'get on with your brother, pay the troops and forget everyone else'. Yet, within a year Caracalla had murdered Geta and executed thousands of his supporters.

Caracalla remained popular with the army because of pay increases, funded by re-organising the coinage. He also widened the tax base by introducing (taxed) citizenship for all free-born men throughout the empire. With some of this money he built the huge Baths of Caracalla in Rome, capable of holding up to 5,000 bathers. Their immense ruins can still be seen.

Caracalla campaigned successfully on the Rhine, and against the Persians in the east. Here he proclaimed himself Alexander the Great, and visited Alexandria to see Alexander's tomb. In a bizarre incident during this visit, his army suddenly turned on the civilian population and slaughtered thousands of them. He was on his way to fight the Persians again in AD 217 when he was assassinated.

Marble bust of Caracalla, who introduced universal citizenship, but murdered his own brother.

Elagabalus (Emperor AD 217 – 222)

After the death of Caracalla, the throne was occupied briefly by Macrinus, the Praetorian commander. He was murdered after a massive defeat by the Persians and a Syrian called Elagabalus profited from the confusion to pass himself off as Caracalla's son. His mother Julia was the power behind the throne, along with her mother, Julia Maesa, the sister-in-law of Septimius Severus.

Elagabalus and his court caused scandal in Rome. The emperor dressed in feminine silk robes, wore make-up and was extremely promiscuous with both sexes, marrying several women, including a Vestal Virgin. He also changed Roman state religion by neglecting Jupiter and building instead an enormous temple of 'Sol Invictus' (the invincible Sun) near the Forum Romanum. In it he placed the sacred black stone of the sun, brought from Syria.

Before long his mother and grandmother quarrelled and Maesa put forward her other grandson, Severus Alexander, to be emperor. The army backed Alexander. Elagabalus and his mother were murdered and their bodies paraded through the streets.

Gold coin of Elegabalus, showing a chariot carrying the sacred black stone of the sun.

Philip 'the Arab' (Emperor AD 244 – 249)

Philip I, known as 'the Arab', was born in south-west Syria. He was a successful general, and in AD 243 defeated the existing emperor, the teenage Gordian III.

But Philip's triumph was short-lived and his reign became one long series of military campaigns against enemies outside and inside the empire. On the eastern frontier he faced the powerful Persian king Shapur. Philip could not beat him and instead had to buy him off with a huge quantity of silver, followed by the promise of yearly payments. Philip then had to turn back to fight against Gothic barbarians who had crossed the River Danube. One of the few bright spots of his reign was in AD 248, when he commemorated the thousandth anniversary of the foundation of Rome with theatrical performances, chariot races and other entertainments. The following year Philip's own generals rebelled against him and Philip was killed. A general called Decius made himself emperor. The empire descended further into chaos.

Gold brooch made with a coin of Philip 'the Arab'.

Gallienus (Emperor AD 253–268)

Decius died fighting the Goths and a Roman aristocrat called Valerian and his son Gallienus became joint Augusti. Their reign included some of the darkest years of Rome's history.

A usurper, Postumus, declared a breakaway 'Gallic empire' of Britain, Spain, France and Germany in the West. In the east, the Persian King Shapur attacked Syria, Turkey and Egypt and captured Valerian. Odenath, ruler of Palmyra in Syria defeated the Persians and recaptured the east, but was murdered, and his empire passed to his widow, Queen Zenobia.

Coin showing Gallienus in military uniform. During his reign the empire nearly fell apart forever.

At home Gallienus made Milan the capital of the empire in AD 256, because of its strategic position near the frontier, and based rapid response units of cavalry in the city. Wars, plague and reorganisations were draining the treasury so Gallienus massively debased the coinage, and inflation rocketed.

War returned in AD 267, when Gothic and Herulian barbarians descended on Greece and Turkey destroying several cities, including Athens. Gallienus defeated them but then faced a rebellion by Danubian generals in Milan. During the siege of the city Gallienus was murdered.

Aurelian (Emperor AD 270 – 275)

Claudius II became emperor and battled successfully against the invaders, but died of plague on campaign in AD 270. He was succeeded by Aurelian, a commander from Moesia (part of modern Croatia), who immediately faced problems on the frontiers. When German tribes invaded Italy, Aurelian forced them out, but saw the very serious threat to Rome, so he built a great defensive wall around the city, still visible today.

In AD 272 he crushed the rebellion of Queen Zenobia of Palmyra who had seized the east and, most importantly, the Egyptian wheat supply. In AD 274 he defeated the breakaway 'Gallic Empire' and regained the west, after which he was hailed as *Restitutor Orbis,* the 'Restorer of the World'. He also passed numerous measures to re-establish the economy and the monetary system and launched a programme of administrative reforms.

In a very short time Aurelian had reunited and strengthened the empire, and reinforced its frontiers, but sadly in AD 275 he was assassinated.

Coin of Aurelian, who fought hard and finally reunited the empire

Diocletian (Emperor AD 284 – 305)

Diocletian came from a poor family in modern Croatia, but rose to be a general, and by AD 284 he had become emperor of the east.

He made his friend and fellow officer Maximian co-Augustus of the west, and in AD 293, to regularise the succession and to confront problems across the empire, from British rebellions to Persian invasions, Diocletian created two Caesars as deputies. Galerius was appointed in the East, with Thessaloniki in Greece as his capital, and Constantius, in the West, based at Trier. The 'Tetrarchy' (rule of four) worked well to begin with, and in AD 296 Constantius recaptured Britain, while in AD 298 Galerius inflicted such a crushing defeat on the Persians that they lay low for forty years. The Tetrarchy worked (if everyone co-operated).

Gold coin of Diocletian, the Balkan general who transformed the empire by dividing it into eastern and western parts.

The army was Diocletian's priority and in AD 297, to combat Christianity's influence, he ordered all soldiers to make pagan sacrifice. From 303 he launched the 'Great Persecution', killing thousands of Christians, including famous military martyrs such as Saint Sebastian. He also reorganised the army into fixed frontier

Diocletian *(Continued)*

Part of Diocletian's palace in Split (modern Croatia). In AD 305 Diocletian abdicated and retired to his palace, preferring gardening to affairs of state.

troops and a mobile field army, and increased the number of soldiers needed, but these reforms were expensive.

The economy was in ruins, so he reformed the coinage and introduced an empire-wide price freeze. To help with administration and tax-collecting (and prevent rebellions) he divided the empire into smaller provinces than before. He created a rigid civil service career structure with many senior posts reserved for the military, so the Senate and Rome lost even more influence and power.

In AD 305, Diocletian abdicated and retired to Split. Maximian also retired, so Constantius and Galerius now became Augusti and chose their own Caesars. But co-operation broke down and in AD 308 Diocletian came out of retirement to resolve the crisis. He then returned to Split, preferring, he said, to grow cabbages rather than run the empire. He died peacefully in his palace in AD 311.

Maxentius (Emperor AD 306 – 312)

Maxentius, Maximian's son, was overlooked in the imperial negotiations of AD 305. So, in AD 306, aided by the Praetorian Guard, he seized Rome and declared himself Augustus of Italy and North Africa and was joined by Maximian. Severus and Galerius, the Augusti of West and East, marched against Maxentius but failed to take Rome.

Maxentius associated himself very strongly with Rome and its old traditions. He beautified the city by restoring Hadrian's Temple of Venus and Rome and constructing the enormous Basilica Nova next to it. For himself he built a villa complex on the Via Appia, complete with a racing circus and a huge mausoleum.

In AD 312 Constantine invaded Italy. At the Milvian Bridge outside Rome, Constantine's troops, with shields bearing the Christian cross that Constantine had seen in a dream, routed Maxentius' army. Maxentius and thousands of his men drowned in the Tiber, Constantine became emperor, and the world changed forever.

Coin of Maxentius. The scene of Romulus, Remus and the she-wolf shows Maxentius' commitment to the traditions of pagan Rome.

Constantine (Emperor AD 307 – 337)

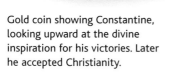

Constantine was the son of Constantius and his first wife Helena. He was with his father in Britain when Constantius died, and in AD 306 Constantine was proclaimed Augustus at Eboracum (York).

At the conference of Carnuntum (near Vienna) in AD 308, Constantine was demoted to Caesar, based at Trier, with Licinius as Augustus. In the east Galerius and Maximinus were Augustus and Caesar, and Maxentius ruled Italy and Africa. After Galerius died in AD 311, Constantine invaded Italy and killed Maxentius. By AD 324 he had killed Licinius and ruled the whole empire.

Gold coin showing Constantine, looking upward at the divine inspiration for his victories. Later he accepted Christianity.

Constantine now moved sharply away from the universal tolerance of his 'Edict of Milan' in AD 313. He outlawed pagan sacrifice, confiscated temple treasuries, and curbed Christian heresies. In AD 325 he called a church synod at Niceaea near Constantinople, which effectively made Christianity the state religion. His mother Helena also promoted Christianity, and made a pilgrimage to the holy land, where she collected relics, identified sacred places and built churches.

Constantine, too, was a great builder. He filled Trier with imperial buildings, and in Rome he built public baths and the great Arch of Constantine near the Colosseum. To thank the Christian God, he also constructed several churches. One, the cathedral church of St John Lateran, was inside the walls, while the others, including the great Basilica of St Peter, were outside, so as not to offend what was still a pagan city.

His greatest project was his 'New Rome' at Byzantium (modern Istanbul). It was dedicated as Constantinople in AD 330, and filled with huge public buildings, squares, palaces, a hippodrome and numerous churches. The creation of this alternative capital formalised a division of the empire that was eventually to tear it in two.

Constantine filled his capital cities with beautiful buildings, such as this great basilica in Trier, Germany.

On the way to campaign against the Persians in AD 337, he died, and was buried in Constantinople. The empire was now a very different place and the future was in the east.

Julian (Emperor AD 361 – 363)

Julian was Constantine's nephew and after his death he fled the massacres at Constantinople that killed his family, and went to study in Athens. The empire was divided between Constantine's three sons, but by AD 352 only Constantius II survived. He sent Julian to the Rhine frontier where he was so popular that Constantius became suspicious of him. He marched against Julian, but died on the way in AD 361.

As sole ruler, Julian wanted to be like great pagan emperors such as Marcus Aurelius. He tried to re-establish paganism by reintroducing animal sacrifice and restoring temple property. He curbed the financial privileges of the Christian church and clergy, and was such a threat that they named him 'Apostate' ('turned from religion'). He also tried to lighten the tax burden by tackling the spiralling costs of government.

Coin showing Julian crowned by the pagan goddess Victory. Julian tried desperately to revive the 'old' religion of pagan Rome.

In AD 363 Julian successfully invaded Persia but was wounded and died. If he had lived longer the history of Rome and of the world would have been very different.

Valentinian I (Emperor AD 364–375)

After Julian's death the army made Jovian emperor, but he died on the way to Constantinople. The Senate and army then chose another general, Valentinian, from Pannonia (modern Serbia), and he made his brother Valens emperor of the East. Once again, warrior generals from the Balkans were in power.

In contrast to many other Christian emperors Valentinian was very tolerant. But society was increasingly polarised between military and aristocracy, east and west, and pagan and Christian, and his attempts at a tolerant compromise were wrecked by war. Tribes such as the Goths and the Alamanni swarmed over the Rhine and the Danube, and in the 'Barbarian Conspiracy' of AD 367 Britain was nearly lost in a wave of revolts and barbarian raids, put down brilliantly by the father of the future emperor Theodosius.

Valentinian was renowned for his fiery temper, and when some barbarian visitors were not, in his eyes, sufficiently respectful, he died of a stroke brought on by sheer rage.

Coin showing Valentinian. Like Julian he is crowned by Victory, but he holds a standard with a Christian Chi-Rho symbol.

Theodosius (Emperor AD 375 – 395)

Valentinian's sons Gratian and Valentinian II now ruled the west, while Valens in the east made a fatal mistake. Desperate for army recruits, he settled thousands of Visigoths inside the empire, but in AD 378 they rebelled and slaughtered the emperor and his army. Theodosius, a Spanish general, became emperor in the east and in AD 387 he defeated the usurper Magnus Maximus, who had murdered Gratian and invaded France and Italy. Theodosius now ruled the whole empire.

An avid Christian, he earned the title 'the Great' through attacks on Christian heresies and paganism. In Milan he was greatly influenced by Bishop Ambrose, and the emperor's public submission to the authority of Ambrose and the church marked a watershed. Soon afterwards, in AD 391, he ordered the permanent closure of all pagan temples.

When he died the empire was divided between his sons Arcadius in the east and Honorius in the west. The division was now permanent, and the old Roman empire was slipping away.

Silver dish from Spain showing Theodosius in imperial splendour between his co-emperors.

46

Honorius (Emperor AD 395 – 423)

During Honorius' reign the frontiers of the empire were continuously pressed and breached. Italy was not secure and Milan had to be abandoned as the imperial residence, in favour of Ravenna in the north-east, safe within a huge area of marshland.

The Visigoths under their king, Alaric, revolted and rampaged through Greece and the Balkans, and in AD 403 they burst into Italy, but Stilicho, the romanised Vandal commander, was able to turn them back. In AD 406 the Rhine froze over and countless Vandals, Franks, Burgundians and other barbarians, poured into the west. Britain, no longer trusting in imperial promises of assistance, declared independence from Rome.

Coin of Honorius, who presided over the disintegration of the western empire and the sack of Rome.

The Porta San Paolo in Rome, showing the defensive towers added by Honorius (in vain).

The west desperately needed to be saved, but in AD 408 Stilicho was executed on (false) charges of secret negotiations with Alaric. On 28th August AD 410 the greatest horror of all occurred, when Alaric and the Visigoths sacked Rome itself. Afterwards, Honorius reasserted Roman power over parts of the west, but the western empire did not have long to live.

Romulus 'Augustulus' (Emperor AD 475 – 476)

After the sack of Rome and the barbarian invasions, the western empire was in total chaos and in AD 455 Valentinian III, the last legitimate emperor, was murdered.

The eastern emperor and Germanic military commanders now controlled Rome and elected a series of puppet emperors, such as Julius Nepos. In AD 475 a Roman general named Orestes deposed Nepos and made his own son Romulus Augustus emperor. Ironically, this weakest and last of the western emperors shared the glorious names of the founders of the empire and of Rome itself.

Suddenly, thousands of Orestes' German mercenaries in Italy demanded a share of the farming land. Orestes said no and marched against them, but the German commander Odoacer killed him and in AD 476 was proclaimed king. He captured Romulus at Ravenna and exiled him to the Bay of Naples, where he acquired the nickname 'Augustulus' (little Augustus). German kings ruled Italy and the remains of the western empire withered away. The only emperor now was in Constantinople, the capital of the eastern (Byzantine) empire, which lasted until AD 1453.

Gold coin showing Romulus Augustus, the last emperor of the west, who died in obscurity.